1st edition / 1. Auflage, 05-2015

Pferdberg, Steven
Tales from Cornucopia
A collection of miner's poems

Illustrations by Stefan Grossmann
Book Layout by Björn Kahlenberg

Map of Cornucopia by Steven Pferdberg,
using graphic elements created by
Tiffany Munro & Daphne Arcadius

Printed and published by /
Herstellung und Verlag:
BoD - Books on Demand, Norderstedt, Germany

ISBN: 9783734787621

(C) 2015 Steven Pferdberg

Steven Pferdberg

# Tales from
# Cornucopia

*A collection of miner's poems*

*Table Of Contents*

## TALES FROM CORNUCOPIA

| | |
|---|---:|
| Introduction | 1 |
| The Ballad Of Spider Frank | 2 |
| Greed's Hungry Gorge | 4 |
| The Horse On The Cliff | 6 |
| Island Of Wonders | 8 |
| Ode To Lava Falls | 12 |
| Ode To Our Lord Of The Mountain | 14 |
| Ode To The Bermudas | 16 |
| The Raft | 17 |
| Song Of The Merry Farmer | 18 |
| Song Of The Seafarers | 20 |
| To Gold | 23 |
| To Iron | 24 |
| The Town And The Spider | 26 |
| The Tree Garden | 30 |

## APPENDIX

| | |
|---|---:|
| Claire Voyant's Secret Notes | 39 |
| Map of Cornucopia | 43 |

*For the citizens of Cornucopia.*

## *Introduction*

I greet thee, hungry traveller,
The name is Pferdberg, Steven.
I like to write about the things
That make me feel uneven.

The rhythms might seem obvious,
The rhymes are sometimes simple.
A poet knows, a face is just
The canvas for a pimple.

## The Ballad Of Spider Frank

Spider Frank was fast and friendly,
Speedy and sincere.
You could give him things to carry,
He would bring them here.

Cobblestone to Little Island,
Jungle Trees to Spider Town,
Homemade bread to hungry travellers,
He would never let us down.

Always keen on looking spiffy,
Saddles, Ee and Aw!
A to B right in a jiffy,
Load and heave and ho!

Then, one night, a greenish devil
Crept along the twilit farm.
Snickered mean, the ever sneaky,
As he snuck into the barn.

Spider Frank was unsuspicious,
Couldn't hear the hissing beast.
He died in the line of duty,
Carrying the baker's yeast.

Hitherto old Frank had never
Met a thing as devious.
Blown to bits, he'll be remembered
Like no donkey previous.

People say he had it coming,
That he'd been an easy prey.
Spider Frank was our dear friend,
And our friends we wish to stay.

Spider Frank was fast and friendly,
Speedy and sincere.
Mem'ries of a fallen comrade,
We will hold them dear.

## Greed's Hungry Gorge

"Begone thy baneful spell!" I clepe.
I will not even bother.
My treasure-ladden bag is full,
I cannot take another.

A precious stone, it greets my eye,
Just there beyond the chasm.
Collecting and retrieving it
Becomes a wild phantasm.

A monkey rideth pickaback,
Temptation is a rotter!
And still my mind congratulates,
I am a skillful spotter.

The greed within presents itself
As merry a companion.
A wise man knows, behind it hides
A devil in a canyon.

In reaching out my trembling hand,
I praise my past endeavours.
"Tarnation and Dodgast!" methinks,
And fall into the crevice.

# TALES FROM CORNUCOPIA

## The Horse On The Cliff

A horse stood on a cliff one day
And gazed onto the plains,
The lands of Cornucopia,
Where Gorf the Golem reigns.

So many roads that lead from here
To unseen magic places!
Which one to take of all the paths?
A horse loves open spaces.

"Along the river I could go."
It thought, and almost vowed it.
Its vision of the river's course
Was vague and somewhat clouded.

"Or up into the mountainscape,
Across the sparkling fountain?"
It knew that it was not well fit
For travelling on the mountain.

"Into the dark oak forest then,
Where mushrooms stand in shadows!
Or South into the desert plains,
Or just into the meadows?"

So many roads that led from there
And so few hours to wander.
Upon all possibilites
This happy horse did ponder.

All suddenly a hand appeared
To tighten strings. Departure!
This freedom-loving horse belonged
To quite a busy archer.

One day, the horse will travel out
To unforeseen directions.
Until then human work awaits,
Experience comes in fractions.

## Island Of Wonders

O island of wonders,
So far out at sea,
Unveileth thy deepest mystery

To four reckless heroes,
United and brave!
Don't judge them on how they
Might sometimes behave.

For travel they must,
Through stark foreign lands,
Their hunger is why they
So slowly advance.

When the comforts of home
Are far far away,
And unfriendly monsters
Don't want them to stay,

Their eyes gazing southward,
Their hearts full of hope,
Not yet do their minds see
With what they must cope.

Beyond all that frightens,
All perils, all doom,
Out there in the sun's
Sweet and peaceful last gloom

Shines faintly an island,
Few men ever saw,
Not bound by all cosmic
Or natural law.

In her solemn golden
And violet glow
Stand cows in strange colors,
And prompt them to bow.

"O give us thy sapid
Yet outlandish stew!
And sing us thy gracious
Yet primitive moo!"

The journey victorious,
Their heads high and bold,
Alas there is hefty
A chapter soon told.

Four left the city,
And just three arrived.
Three went through fire,
But just one survived.

But powers mysterious,
From ages long gone,
Them granted a respawn
And strength to move on.

As night shrouds the city,
Comradery prevails.
Our heroes return
And live to tell tales.

## Ode To Lava Falls

O have ye wandered
To Lava Falls nigh?
Where the blood of the Earth
Falls from the sky,

Where heroes go fishing
By the starlit lagoon,
And architects run out
Of spruce wood too soon.

Where an old haunted hotel
Sits gently with birch,
And treacherous magma
Flows right through a church.

Where infinite tunnels
Host many a gem,
And cows even smile,
Being turned into ham.

Where climbers crouch low
And divers fly high,
And enchanted arrows
Kiss creepers good-bye.

So wander, ye traveller,
While skies are still blue!
The town of Lava Falls
Has a guest bed for you.

## Ode To Our Lord Of The Mountain

Winged you stand
On top of the hill,
The shining river beneath your feet.

The eternal streams,
That fall from the hill,
You watch over them, day and night.

Without them we'd thirst,
And our crops would be bleak,
But you bless the streams, and we see it.

With firm grip you hold
The torch high and bold,
That enlightens the town we recieved.

Bless the villagers with hope,
They'll fight in the swamp,
Faithful they'll have what they need.

# TALES FROM CORNUCOPIA

## Ode To The Bermudas

Where once stood a temple,
You stand above clouds.
Beneath dwell the divers,
Surround the lighthouse.

Refreshened by potions
A smiling man brewed,
Forget introductions,
You're now known as "dude".

Sad spikefish is screeching,
You just hold the wire,
As soon it will enter
The chamber of fire.

The soft sandy beaches,
A vast fruit buffet,
Cows greet from the boat bridge,
Then swim round the bay.

Occasional rainfall
Can't spoil the great vibe.
Welcome to the island!
Welcome to the tribe!

## The Raft

I crafted a raft
Without any draft.

It wasn't that hard,
Not unlike a cart.

Have well understood:
Save iron! Take wood!

Then take to the seas,
Be full of ideas.

## Song Of The Merry Farmer

O merry the farmer
Who never forgets,
What you take from the land
Is just temporarily yours.

He greets the old dog,
Who sits on his steps,
For he too understands,
What's given is given for good.

The clock on the shelf
Sings a salute
To the scars on his hands,
But the rhythm is peaceful at last.

Summer will come
On a horse that won't kneel,
And the smallest of grains
Is delightful to hold in his hands.

# TALES FROM CORNUCOPIA

## Song Of The Seafarers

Lightning bolt and thunderclap
Rage across the sky. (Hey!)
Safe and sound we ride the waves,
Over the sea we fly. (Hey!)

The Eastern Sea, the Western Sea
And everywhere in between. (Hey!)
We belong under open skies,
So that's where we'll be seen. (Hey!)

We pity the adventurer,
Who left his brews his home. (Hey!)
Let's all take a breath and dive
To the mystic dome. (Hey!)

Evil fish and guardians,
Hear them all complain. (Hey!)
We are here to fight and steal
Precious porcelain. (Hey!)

Round the Cape Croissant we go,
Wienerfell is near. (Hey!)
Clouds are looming o'er our heads, but
Soon the skies will clear. (Hey!)

Summon a drink and gather round,
The shore is nigh in sight. (Hey!)
Sail we will, through days of lore
And through darkest night. (Hey!)

Lightning bolt and thunderclap
Rage across the sky. (Hey!)
Safe and sound we ride the waves,
Over the sea we fly. (Hey!)

# TALES FROM CORNUCOPIA

## To Gold

O gold!

What lovely serendipity
That puts me in thy presence!
Thy shine it is that separates
Us noblemen from peasants.

The weaponsmith is not impressed,
And neither are the hecklers.
I will not take their words to heart,
I'll wear thee as a necklace!

## To Iron

O iron!

Thy auspicious silver gleaming,
Thy sweet old familiar face!
For thee in my dusty pockets
I will always find a space.

Hidden under stone for ages,
Sunlight now caresses thee.
Prisoned in these walls forever,
I will help thee to break free.

Now thy glistering visage
Changes, thrust into the flames.
Molten into swords and axes,
Gaia gives what man reclaims.

Thou empowerest us to fight our
Enemies and overlords,
With thee by our side, we fear not
Ghastly ghouls nor savage hordes.

Settlers praise thee, travellers need thee,
Thou art tough and rare to splice.
And upon thy trusted nature
Our survival still relies.

# TALES FROM CORNUCOPIA

## TALES FROM CORNUCOPIA

### *The Town And The Spider*

Long ago, a spider came
Across a swampy valley.
Found a town that was just three
Houses and an alley.

Tasty humans crawled around,
Panicking and shrieking.
Hungry spider was confused:
Food buffets are freaking?

Hastily it went away,
To a nearby mountain,
Had to find another meal,
Tourists aren't counting.

Chanced upon a spider girl,
Witty and attractive.
Eight-legged civilization things
Came into perspective.

Mineshaft full of working folk,
Busy and distracted,
Spider laughed and ate them all,
Soldiers were contracted.

Suddenly a hero stood
Grinning on the bedrock,
Wielding shiny diamond arms,
Offspring of the townsfolk.

Hungry spider, angry man
And a score to settle.
Maybe you can guess who won
This historic battle.

Dagger 'tween the eyeballs and
Claws on human faces,
Things got out of hand quite fast,
Caves are violent spaces.

Duel in the dark, the odds
Even and in balance.
Hero waved about his sword
'Tween two fearful seconds.

Wounded beast collapsed and slid
From a small protrusion,
As this hungry spider's tale
Comes to its conclusion.

Glorious day of victory,
Massive celebration,
Carcass in the central square,
Death of spider nation.

Laughing people, posing with
Boots on dead beast's forehead.
How could God create a wild
Animal so horrid?

Cornucopia's oldest town,
Honest and medieval,
Once infested, now reclaimed,
Free from beasts primeval.

# TALES FROM CORNUCOPIA

## The Tree Garden

If you look at them from far away,
A peaceful dance of shadows,
A seascape with a hundred sails,
All scattered on the meadows.

But when you go, as night falls down,
Prepare your evening pillows,
Hush! And you will notice that
There's whisper in the willows.

In gallant robes of green they move
And gather by a campsite.
A new bloom has grown on their land,
Competing for the sunlight.

The dark oak lifts his head up high
And has his crown adjusted.
With solemn voice he boldly speaks:
"They are not to be trusted."

He recalls recent massacres,
Remembers friends combusted,
Whole family lines were hacked to shreds,
Some spruces look disgusted.

Who is this unseen enemy?
What drives it to such cruelty?
To stand and fight back this new threat
All take an oath of fealty.

The duke of spruces rises up
And takes the floor, all gallant.
To summon words of bravery
He had a special talent.

"They've made a weapon we can't fight,
That's custom-made to kill us:
A shiny blade with evil grin,
A brachial bacillus."

"My fellow trees, they swiftly rush
through our midst and slay us,
We have to make a move on them,
Or else they will betray us."

"The corpses of our friends and foes,
Stacked up in grotesque manner.
All different tribes of trees must now
Unite under one banner!"

Their manes sway softly in the wind,
All nod in quiet approval.
Trees serious and dignified,
Awaiting their removal.

The birch, all bashful, lifts her head
And makes a shy confession:
"The two-legged folks, with all their faults,
They're masters of progression."

An uproar shakes the canopy,
Outragéd angry rustle.
"Explain yourself, young birchen friend,
Or feel my wooden muscle!"

The birch, all pensive for a while,
considers how to highlight
There is some good in humankind,
Albeit sometimes in twilight.

"They plant young saplings, water them,
Make sure they are promoted.
Without them, would we be here now,
On soil that lay eroded?"

A few trees nod, most shake their heads,
There's murmur, fissling, splutter.
The birch, she stands alone with few,
Most trees still vote for slaughter.

"An era where we face our end
Is not the time for truces.
We have to fight and not look back."
So speaks the duke of spruces.

The night becomes decidual
And ends in wild confusion.
As sunlight peeks around the hill,
There is no clear conclusion.

The human kind, a mystery
To beings of wood and leaves.
What creature would both plant the seed,
Then kill what it recieves?

Our spirit and our gentleness,
It is from them not hidden.
Our briefness and barbarity,
They've seen the horse it's ridden.

They look like they're not moving much,
You think they can't be thinking.
While we haste after daily dues,
The hearts of trees are sinking.

They wonder who on Earth we are,
And what's our common praxis?
What will we bring when we return,
Our bonemeal or our axes?

# TALES FROM CORNUCOPIA

# APPENDIX

*Claire Voyant's Secret Notes*

There is a strange presence in the birch forest north of Dead Spider Valley. I sense a familiar force, but I'm not sure if it is one of those that should be trusted.

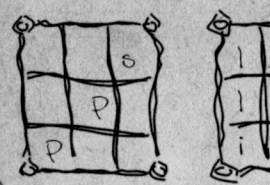

I sense that this country will be overrun by tourists soon. Coincidentally, I haven't seem my brother for quite some time. I wonder if he has anything to do with all these people arriving here lately...

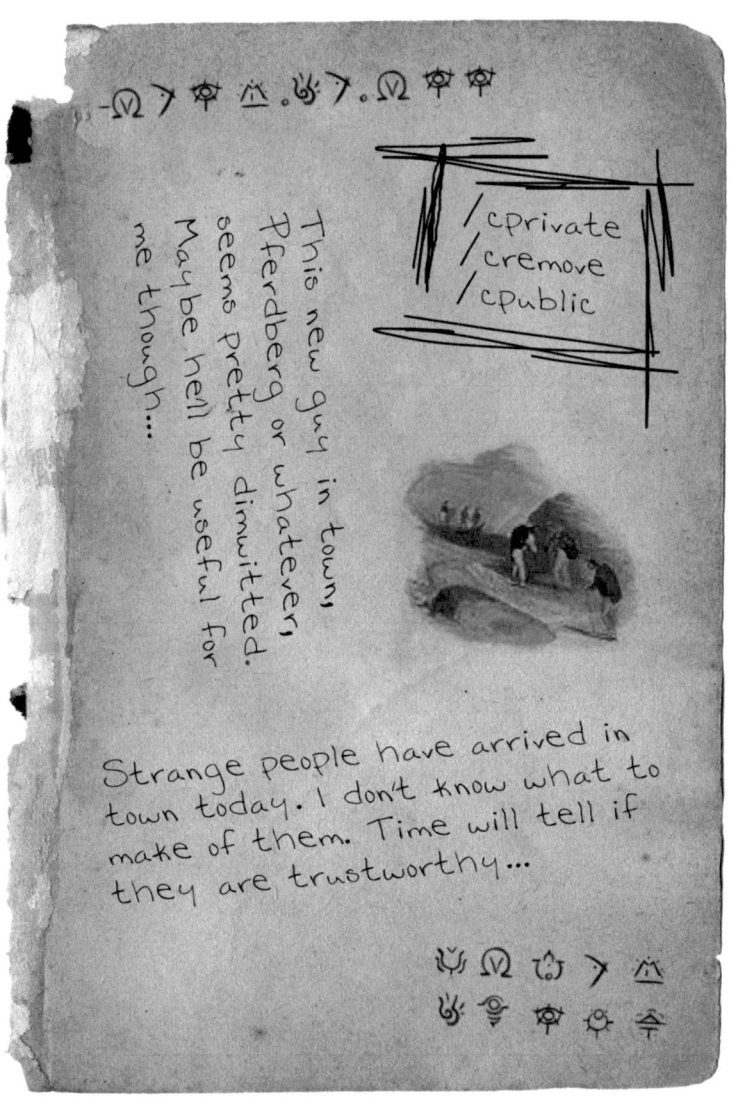

This new guy in town, Pferdberg or whatever, seems pretty dimwitted. Maybe he'll be useful for me though...

/cprivate
/cremove
/cpublic

Strange people have arrived in town today. I don't know what to make of them. Time will tell if they are trustworthy...

*Map of Cornucopia*

# TALES FROM CORNUCOPIA

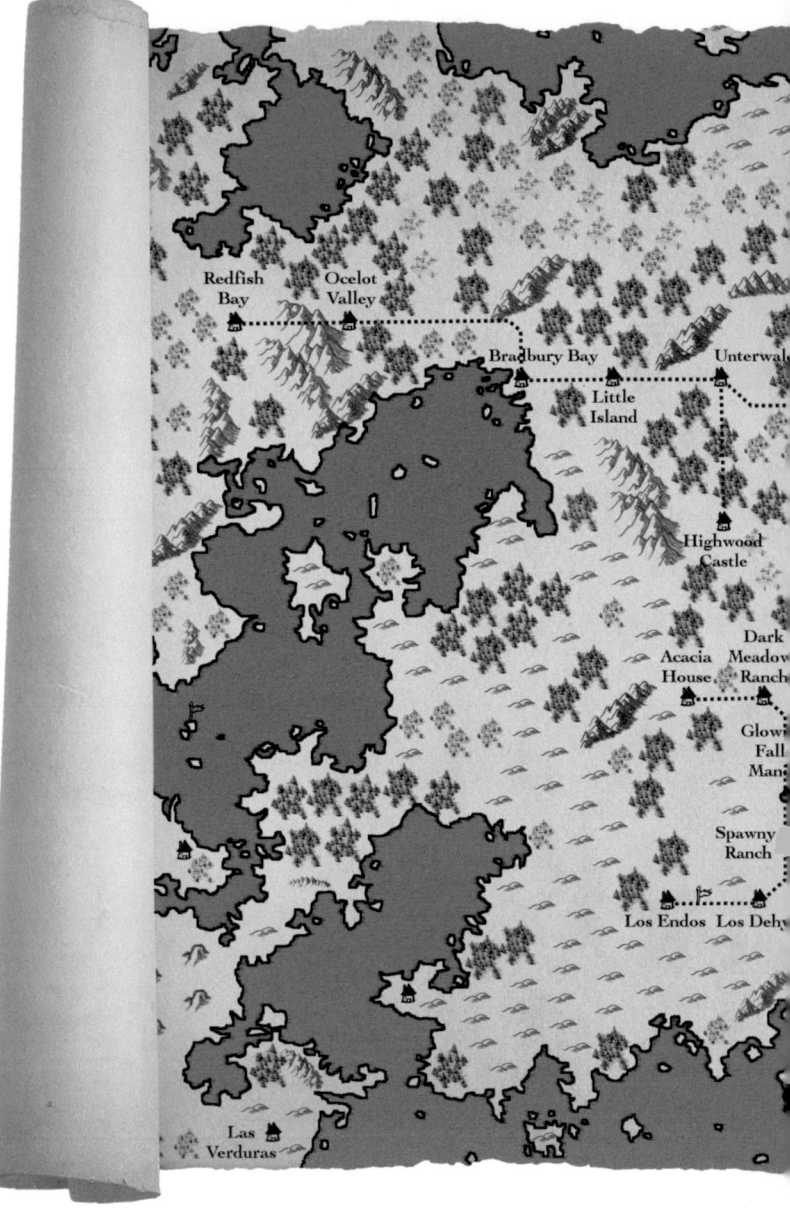

# TALES FROM CORNUCOPIA

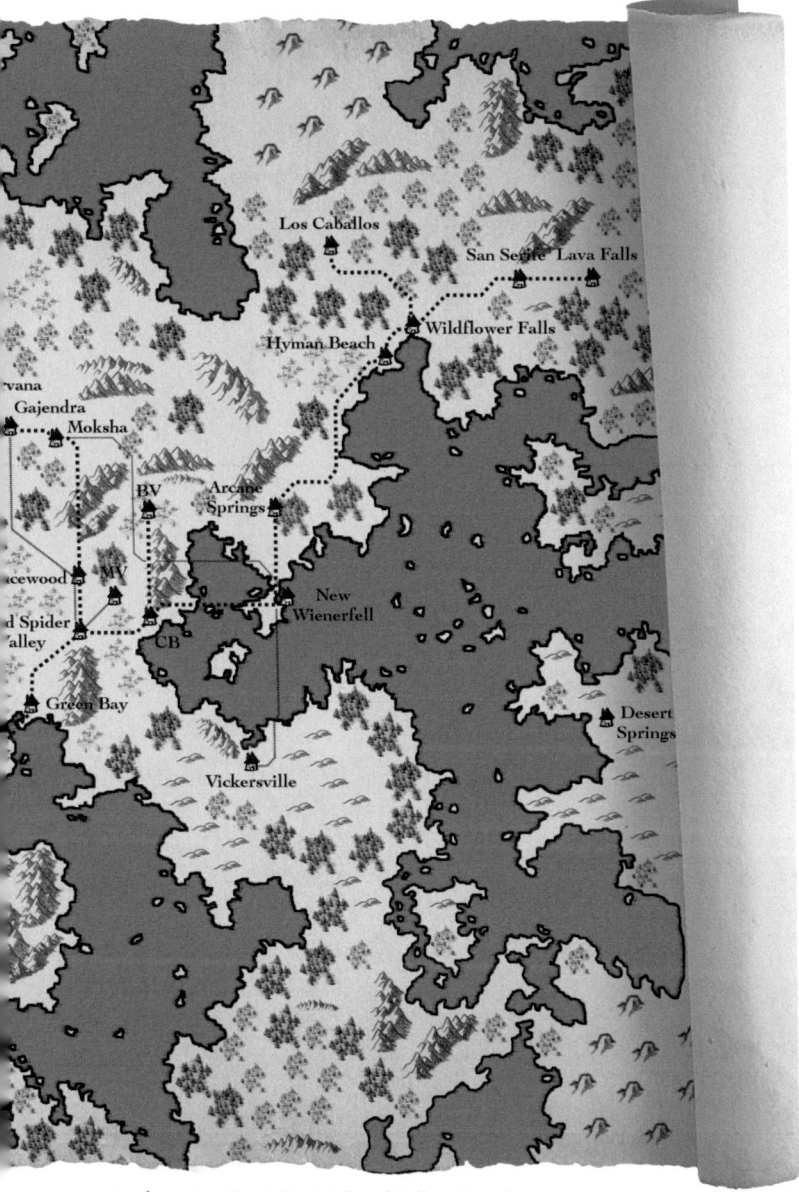

BV = Birchwood Valley, MV = Medieval Valley, CB = Cappuccino Bay

## TALES FROM CORNUCOPIA

*Personal Notes:*